Facts About the Walrus

By Lisa Strattin

© 2019 Lisa Strattin

FREE BOOK

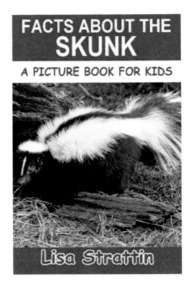

BOX SET

- **FACTS ABOUT THE POISON DART FROGS**
- **FACTS ABOUT THE THREE TOED SLOTH**
- **FACTS ABOUT THE RED PANDA**
- **FACTS ABOUT THE SEAHORSE**
- **FACTS ABOUT THE PLATYPUS**
- **FACTS ABOUT THE REINDEER**
- **FACTS ABOUT THE PANTHER**
- **FACTS ABOUT THE SIBERIAN HUSKY**

LisaStrattin.com/BookBundle

Facts for Kids Picture Books by Lisa Strattin

Little Blue Penguin, Vol 92

Chipmunk, Vol 5

Frilled Lizard, Vol 39

Blue and Gold Macaw, Vol 13

Poison Dart Frogs, Vol 50

Blue Tarantula, Vol 115

African Elephants, Vol 8

Amur Leopard, Vol 89

Sabre Tooth Tiger, Vol 167

Baboon, Vol 174

Sign Up for New Release Emails Here

LisaStrattin.com/subscribe-here

Contents

INTRODUCTION

The Walrus is a large marine mammal found living in the cold and icy waters of the Arctic Circle. Thought to be most closely related to Fur Seals, they are the second largest ocean-dwelling mammals that come ashore to breed. Only the Elephant Seals are larger. Walruses are highly distinctive among the pinnipeds because of their sensitive whiskers and long tusks.

There are two species of walrus that vary slightly in appearance but mostly differ in the geographic location where they live, the Atlantic Walrus and the Pacific Walrus. It is widely debated that there might be a third species known as the Laptev Walrus that is found only in the Laptev Sea. Many believe these are simply a population of Pacific Walruses that specifically live in this area.

CHARACTERISTICS

Walruses are very sociable animals living in large herds on the ice floes. These herds can contain up to thousands of individual animals and consist mainly of females, called cows, with their young, along with a smaller number of dominant males, which are called bulls. When they retreat into the water to feed, the herds break up into smaller groups numbering as few as ten so there is less competition for food. They are known to make a variety of vocal sounds including loud bellows during the mating season that are produced using the two pouches of air in their necks.

They are well adapted to living in some of the coldest regions in the world with a thick skin that covers a thick layer of blubber, or fat. This helps to keep them warm. Their enormous tusks are known to establish an individual's social status and even help them with balancing and getting around. They dig their tusks into ice floes to help them pull out of the water and also anchor their tusks into the ice so that they can sleep with their bodies submerged beneath the waves. Walruses are also known to use their tusks like a pick-axe to carve their way through the thick ice.

APPEARANCE

Walruses have large, elongated bodies that are wider at the head and neck and taper slimmer toward their tail. Their tough, wrinkled skin is covered by a layer of coarse hairs and is usually grey or brown. However, when they are sunbathing on land or on an ice floe, the skin of the Walrus develops a pink-red color.

They have two pairs of flippers that are used to propel them through the water. Their bodies are powered by their back flippers while the front flippers are used to steer them in the right direction. On land, they move clumsily on all fours, curling their back flippers underneath them to provide more support.

REPRODUCTION

Walruses breed in the middle of winter between the months of January and March. After a gestation period of around 15 months, a single pup is born (on the ice) measuring up to 4 feet long and weighing around 150 pounds!

Walrus pups have short, soft hair covering their bodies, pale grey flippers and a thick, white moustache with no visible teeth. They drink their mother's milk for their first six months, then they begin to eat more solid foods. After their first year, the pups are almost triple the size they were at birth and begin to become more and more independent. They still tend to remain close to their mothers until they are two or three years old.

Young females will often stay close to their mother much longer, but the males begin to move away from the herd to join all-male bachelor groups. Females are able to reproduce at around 6 or 7 years of age but males are not mature until they are at least 10 years old. However, males must prove their dominance over other males in order to mate, and often are not able to do this until they are about 15 years of age.

LIFE SPAN

A walrus lives for 40 to 50 years.

SIZE

Adults tend to be 7.5 to 10.5 feet long on average and weigh between 850 and 3,500 pounds!

Males are generally double the weight of their female counterparts and have much longer tusks.

HABITAT

Walruses are found throughout the northern Atlantic and Pacific Oceans where they live on the ice floes and rocky coastlines. They also spend a lot of time in the freezing cold water. During the winter months when the ice is thickest, they prefer areas of thinner ice so that they can easily break through to the surface from the water below. In the warmer summer months, they can be found commonly on remote areas of rocky coastline.

Despite being well suited to the freezing conditions in the far north, they have been known to move further south into areas of Central Canada, around the United Kingdom and even as far away as the waters close to the Spanish coast.

They do spend most of their time in and around the Arctic Circle.

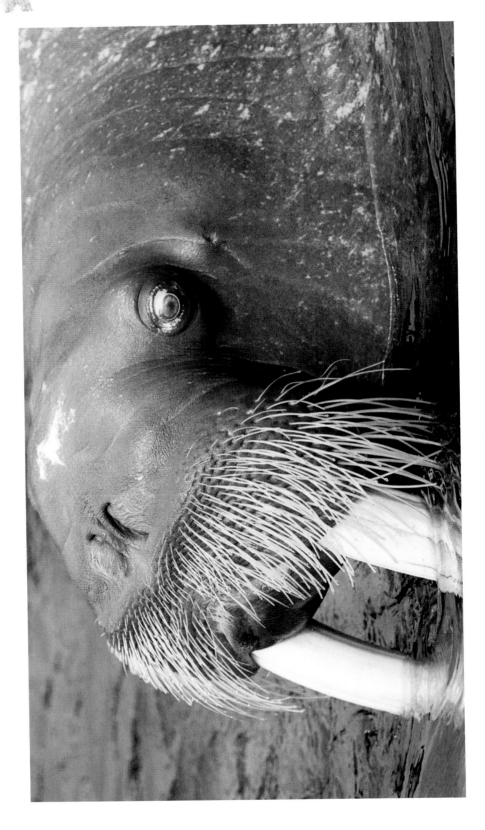

DIET

Walruses are carnivorous animals that only hunt and eat other animals to survive. They have a thick moustache that has about 450 sensitive whiskers that help them to find food in the dark and murky waters at depths of more than 100 yards (over 300 feet) below the surface. They get almost all of their prey from the ocean floor and are known to shoot streams of both air and water into the sediment to find food hidden under the sand.

Walruses feed on a variety of different prey including: clams, snails, worms, squid, octopuses and even some slow-moving fish. Some walrus populations are also known to hunt seals.

ENEMIES

Due to the large size and aggressive nature of these mammals, walruses have only a few predators in their natural environments. Pods of Killer Whales and the occasional Polar Bear are enemies, but they can easily defend themselves with their tusks.

SUITABILITY AS PETS

These are animals that you should visit in a zoo or marine habitat. You might have to do some research to find a place that has built the appropriate enclosure for them, but if you have a zoo or aquarium that houses them nearby, you will enjoy visiting them.

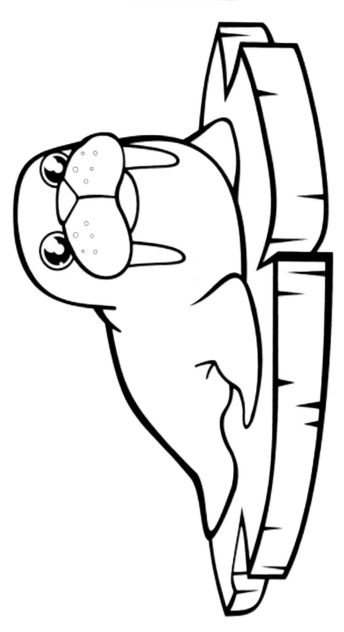

COLOR ME

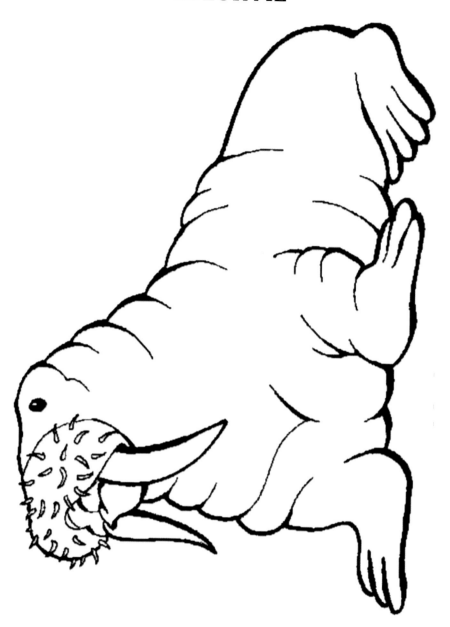

COLOR ME

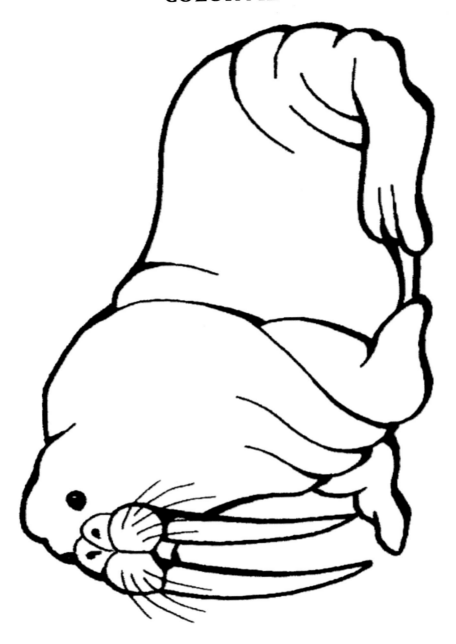

COLOR ME

COLOR ME

COLOR ME

COLOR ME

COLOR ME

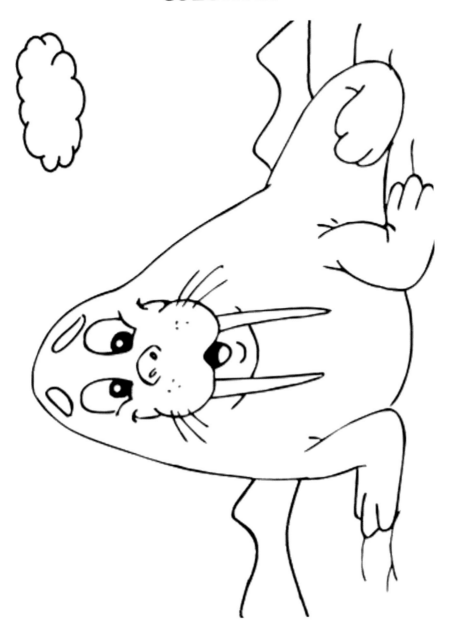

Please leave me a review here:

LisaStrattin.com/Review-Vol-253

For more Kindle Downloads Visit Lisa Strattin
Author Page on Amazon Author Central

amazon.com/author/lisastrattin

To see upcoming titles, visit my website at
LisaStrattin.com– most books available on Kindle!

LisaStrattin.com

FREE BOOK

FOR ALL SUBSCRIBERS – SIGN UP NOW

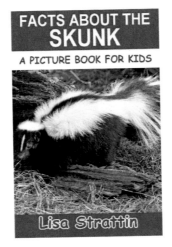

LisaStrattin.com/Subscribe-Here

LisaStrattin.com/Facebook

LisaStrattin.com/Youtube

Made in the USA
Coppell, TX
05 April 2022

76095357R00026